WOMEN IN
THE **WORKPLACE**

BY TAMMY GAGNE

ReferencePoint
Press®

San Diego, CA

LIBRARY OF CONGRESS CATALOGING-IN-PUBLICATION DATA

Names: Gagne, Tammy, author.
Title: Women in the workplace / by Tammy Gagne.
Description: San Diego, CA : ReferencePoint Press, Inc., [2019] | Series:
   Women and society | Audience: Grade 9 to 12. | Includes bibliographical
   references and index.
Identifiers: LCCN 2018046821 (print) | LCCN 2018049148 (ebook) | ISBN
   9781682825549 (ebook) | ISBN 9781682825532 (hardback)
Subjects: LCSH: Women--Employment--Juvenile literature. | Sex discrimination
   in employment--Juvenile literature. | Sex role in the work
   environment--Juvenile literature.
Classification: LCC HD6053 (ebook) | LCC HD6053 .G34 2019 (print) | DDC
   331.4--dc23
LC record available at https://lccn.loc.gov/2018046821

CONTENTS

IMPORTANT EVENTS IN
WOMEN'S HISTORY

1916
Jeannette Rankin of Montana becomes the first woman elected to the US House of Representatives.

1973
The Supreme Court bans gender-based discrimination in advertising for job applicants.

1849
Elizabeth Blackwell becomes the first woman admitted to medical school in the United States.

1932
Hattie Wyatt Caraway of Arkansas becomes the first woman elected to the US Senate.

1860   **1890**   **1920**   **1950**   **1980**

1869
Lemma Barkaloo and Phoebe Wilson Couzins become the first women admitted to law school in the United States.

1920
The Nineteenth Amendment to the US Constitution grants women the right to vote.

1978
The Pregnancy Discrimination Act bans employment discrimination against pregnant women.

1968
Shirley Chisholm becomes the first African American woman elected to the US Congress.

1981
Sandra Day O'Connor becomes the first female justice appointed to the US Supreme Court.

1982
The proposed Equal Rights Amendment, guaranteeing equal rights regardless of sex, fails to become law when only thirty-five states ratify it.

2007
Nancy Pelosi becomes the United States' first female Speaker of the House.

2016
Hillary Rodham Clinton becomes the first female presidential candidate nominated by a major political party in the United States.

1985   **1990**   **2000**   **2010**   **2020**

1983
Sally Ride becomes the first female astronaut from the United States to travel to space.

2013
The United States military removes its ban on female soldiers in combat.

2018
Stacey Cunningham is appointed as the first female president of the New York Stock Exchange.

1985
Wilma Mankiller becomes the first female chief of the Cherokee Nation of Oklahoma.

1997
Madeleine Albright becomes the first female US Secretary of State.

2017
Time magazine names "the Silence Breakers"—women who spoke out in the #MeToo movement against sexual harassment—as its 2017 Persons of the Year.

WORKING
WOMEN

Ursula Burns grew up as the middle child of a single, black mother of three. Her family was not wealthy. They lived in low-income housing on the Lower East Side of Manhattan. Her mother worked hard to make ends meet, running an in-home daycare and taking on odd cleaning jobs to help pay for her children's education. Burns was a bright girl who loved math, which led to a passion for engineering. "I was an oddity in a sea of predominantly white males," Burns has said of her time in high school.[1] Following her graduation, she began working toward a bachelor's degree in mechanical engineering from the Polytechnic Institute of New York University. She eventually earned a master's degree from Columbia University.

Burns started her career with an internship at the printing technology company Xerox in 1980. Then she worked her way up—all the way up. In 2009, she became Xerox's chief executive officer (CEO), making her the first black woman to become the CEO of a *Fortune* 500 company. The *Fortune* 500 is a list of the 500 US corporations with the highest revenues.

Ursula Burns, former CEO of Xerox, speaks at events to help encourage women to pursue their professional goals. As CEO of Xerox, Burns was the first black woman to lead a *Fortune* 500 company.

Burns inherited her mother's strong work ethic, and it clearly paid off. In a 2017 interview, Burns said, "I have more money than my mother would have ever imagined, and I still don't judge my success by that."[2]

Burns has said that making it to the top was not easy. It required a good education, a lot of hard work, and help from others along the way. Burns knows how important these things are to other women working their way up the corporate ladder today, so she donates a great deal of her time to working with organizations that help other women reach their career goals.

Burns' story is just one of many that highlight the enormous strides women have made in the workplace over the last century. Just a few decades before Burns began leading Xerox, women were still fighting to be included in careers that were dominated by men. One of these careers was law enforcement.

In 1975, Brenda Mieth received a rejection letter after she applied for a position as an Alabama state trooper. It said that she did not meet the minimum height and body weight—five-foot-nine-inches (1.75 m) and 160 pounds (72.6 kg)—for the job. Mieth was five-foot-six (1.68 m) and weighed 130 pounds (58.9 kg), but she was determined to not let something so superficial stop her from achieving her goals. She met or exceeded every other requirement for the job. She requested a meeting with the person in charge, hoping to convince him that she would be a good state trooper despite weighing less than the male troopers.

Colonel E. C. Dothard was the head of Alabama's Department of Public Safety. State law gave Dothard the power to waive the weight requirement, but he was not interested in doing so for Mieth. In fact, he openly told her that he would never hire a woman as a state trooper. He believed only men could perform the job due to its dangerous nature. To add insult to injury, Dothard was condescending. "With a flourish, he produced a certificate and handed it to her. It named Mieth an 'Honorary State Trooper,'" explained Gillian Thomas in her book *Because of Sex: One Law, Ten Cases, and Fifty Years That Changed American Women's Lives at Work*.[3] Mieth was not the first woman Dothard had dismissed using size as an excuse. Knowing that the requirements for height and weight were arbitrary, Mieth and another woman filed a lawsuit against Dothard in 1976, claiming that he had discriminated against them based on their gender. The case went all the way to the US Supreme Court, which ruled in favor of the two women.

The Supreme Court's decision helped pave the way for other women who wanted to work in law enforcement, such as Glenda Deese. In addition to being a woman of slight build, Deese was black. This made it doubly difficult for her to gain entry into Alabama's state police department at the time. But another lawsuit in the 1970s addressed this problem. It led to a requirement for Alabama state troopers to hire and promote qualified African Americans. In 1980, Deese became the state's first black female trooper cadet. She eventually became the second-highest-ranking official in the Alabama Department of Public Safety. Deese said, "I just focused on working hard and being the best I could be. All I needed was an opportunity to prove myself."[4]

ONGOING CHALLENGES

However, it seems that for every victory and for every barrier beaten down, women continued to face hurdles in the workplace throughout history. If they weren't fighting discrimination to simply get into jobs, they were often met with harassment from their male supervisors and colleagues. Many women have also had to work harder for less pay than their male counterparts in the workforce. Some men—and even some fellow women—have viewed women as weaker or otherwise less than their male coworkers for being wives and mothers in addition to working their jobs. Although women have made enormous strides in all of these areas compared to when they first joined the workforce, many problems persist. The United States has yet to achieve equal representation in top positions of the workforce—from private companies to the US Supreme Court. And despite the fact that many other nations of the world have female leaders, the United States had never elected a female president through 2019. As Bryce Covert wrote in an article for *Forbes* magazine, "The rest of the world has stayed dynamic and adapted to the increasingly female face of the workforce. The U.S., on the other hand, has stayed stuck. Our barely adequate policies of the 1990s have failed to keep up with women's continuing desire to enter the workforce, which means we're shooting ourselves in the female foot."[5]

"The rest of the world has stayed dynamic and adapted to the increasingly female face of the workforce. The U.S., on the other hand, has stayed stuck. Our barely adequate policies of the 1990s have failed to keep up with women's continuing desire to enter the workforce, which means we're shooting ourselves in the female foot."

– *Bryce Covert, writer*

CHAPTER ONE

WHAT IS THE HISTORY BEHIND WOMEN IN **THE WORKPLACE?**

||||

It is not unusual to find women in nearly every part of the workforce today. Upon entering essentially any business—from a fast food restaurant to an insurance company, it is common to see female employees hard at work. Women perform a wide variety of jobs throughout the United States and other industrialized nations, including entry-level positions, management, and, at certain companies, top executive positions. By 2010, women made up more than 40 percent of the workforce in more than eighty countries. But this was not always the case. For much of history, most women were limited to familial roles in society, spending their time as wives and mothers. Their primary job was to care for their homes, husbands, and children.

When the Industrial Revolution began during the eighteenth century, businesses gained the ability to manufacture textiles and other products faster than ever before. This was thanks to the invention of machinery such as the power loom. Before this time, household linens and garments were made by hand, most often in people's homes. This new era gave

Today, women make up almost half of the American workforce, with jobs in all settings, from factories to restaurants to corporate offices. However, in the past, women were excluded from the workforce.

women another way to help their families. After learning how to operate power looms and other new machinery, women joined the working class by taking jobs in textile mills and other types of factories. These jobs typically based employees' pay on the quantity of goods they produced— but women, like the children who also worked in these factories, were not paid as much as the men performing the same factory jobs. All employees were expected to work in unsafe conditions for unreasonably long hours, effectively making these businesses the first sweatshops. Although they were far from ideal opportunities, these factory positions were among the first jobs outside the home held by many women.

Some historians point out that women were part of the workforce long before the dawn of the Industrial Revolution, performing physical labor on family farms in addition to domestic tasks in their homes. Although farm work was arduous, it came with a silver lining. As Amy Mattson Lauters discusses in her book, *More Than a Farmer's Wife: Voices of the American Farm Women, 1910–1960*, many women who engaged in farming with their husbands saw themselves as equal partners in the endeavor. Lauters wrote that these women "kept the farm's financial accounts and were as adept at running the farm as they were at running the farm home."[6]

Farming became less and less common as time went on, however. Around the beginning of the twentieth century, about 36 percent of families in the United States still participated in agriculture as a means of supporting themselves. By the 1980s, however, the number of US families with farms had dropped to just 3 percent. It was during this century that the number of women in the workplace began to rise again.

THE FIRST JOBS HELD BY WOMEN

During the nineteenth century, and even near the beginning of the twentieth century, the jobs available to women were rather limited. If a woman worked outside her home, it was common for her to be employed as a domestic servant, such as a cook or a maid, in a wealthy household. Before the Thirteenth Amendment abolished slavery in 1865, black women in the United States were not even paid in these positions.

Before women got jobs outside of their homes during the Industrial Revolution, many worked on their family farms. This included physical labor in addition to their household chores.

Enslaved women who did not work inside slaveholders' houses were usually forced to work in the fields.

By 1911, more than a million working women in England and Wales were domestic servants. These women were using the skills they had learned at home to work in the homes of others. Many middle-class

In the 1800s, teaching became one of the first female-dominated jobs. As men pursued higher-paying careers, open teaching jobs created an opportunity for women to educate themselves and work outside of their homes.

women and nearly all female members of the upper class in both the United States and the United Kingdom still did not work, though. The ones who did typically served as in-home schoolteachers or music teachers.

Teaching, although now a common profession among women, did not start out that way. For many years nearly all teachers were men.

Between the 1820s and 1830s, education became more available to the masses as more and more common schools, or early versions of public schools, were established. Before this time, education was considered a privilege for upper-class people who could afford to attend private learning institutions. All the new schools needed teachers, but the number of men interested in teaching decreased as young men started gravitating toward more prestigious and better-paying jobs, such as those in law and medicine. The solution to this problem, proposed by pioneers of education such as Catharine Beecher and Mary Lyon, was to allow more women to become teachers. "[Students of these education pioneers] gathered in schools and literary societies to test the proposition that women's intellects were, in fact, equal to men's," Lori D. Ginzberg writes in her book *Elizabeth Cady Stanton: An American Life*.[7]

Teaching, perhaps more than any other profession open to women during this era, offered young women the opportunity to educate themselves. Although female teachers were at first outsiders in the profession, they quickly realized they had a great resource in one another and formed associations with other women who were new to teaching. These connections allowed women to share ideas and build confidence in a job that until then many people thought women could not, or should not, perform. Through this process and their growing numbers, female teachers were able to start changing attitudes about women in the workplace.

The types of jobs for which women were commonly hired expanded a bit in 1874 and again in 1876, when the typewriter and the telephone, respectively, became the latest technologies in the workplace. One of the first companies to sell typewriters on a large scale was Remington. "They produced beautiful [advertisements] with attractive women typing away," says Alex Werner, head of collections at the Museum of London, which owns a collection of the earliest typewriter models.[8] Marketing campaigns like the one Werner describes aimed to reach more women interested in working outside the home—and they were effective.

Working as secretaries and receptionists, women were now at the forefront of many businesses, if only in the literal sense: They were the first point of contact most people had with a business because these women were the ones greeting clients at the door and answering the phone. Secretarial work typically paid as much as teaching jobs at this time. Although the personal computer and other electronic gadgets have made the typewriter obsolete in modern offices, women have continued to be the predominant workers in secretarial positions.

NO WOMEN ALLOWED

As a handful of professions started opening doors to women, many other jobs were still rejecting all female candidates. If a woman wanted to become a doctor or a lawyer, her aspirations were often ignored or even met with laughter or disdain by the men who dominated these professions for much of the nineteenth century. One of the biggest obstacles was the lack of higher education available to women. While young men were studying law and medicine at prestigious universities, women were restricted from the formal academic setting.

Elizabeth Blackwell moved to the United States with her family from England in 1832, when she was just eleven years old. A prolific student, Blackwell was inspired by a dying friend to pursue a career as a doctor. But whenever she shared her ambition, others told her that it was an impossible dream for a woman. In addition to her great intellect and her desire to help the sick, Blackwell also possessed a strong urge to break through the barriers that kept women from joining the ranks of men in the workplace. She wrote in her diary, "The idea of winning a doctor's degree gradually assumed the aspect of a great moral struggle, and the moral fight possessed immense attraction for me."[9]

Elizabeth Blackwell was the first woman admitted to medical school in the United States. She graduated at the top of her class and eventually started an all-woman medical school.

Blackwell applied to four of the best medical schools in the country, but all four swiftly rejected her. Blackwell did not let these setbacks keep her from her goal. She went on to apply to a total of twenty-nine schools, but she received rejections from each one. Still, she did not give up.

Eventually, she was accepted to Geneva Medical College in New York. As the first woman admitted to a medical school in the United States, she earned her degree in 1849, graduating at the top of her class.

Despite her hard-won successes, no one in the medical community would hire Blackwell. She even traveled back to England in search of work, but she had no luck finding a job as a doctor there either. Blackwell had worked as a teacher to save the money she needed for medical school. This background in education, combined with her medical knowledge, led her to start a school of her own when she returned to the United States. It was the Woman's Medical College of the New York Infirmary, the first medical school in the country dedicated to training women to become doctors.

Education also proved to be a difficult barrier for women interested in becoming lawyers. Arabella Mansfield never attended law school. Instead, she studied alongside her husband, who was also preparing to enter the field of law. Mansfield became the first woman certified to practice law in the United States when she passed the Iowa bar exam in 1869. That same year, Lemma Barkaloo and Phoebe Wilson Couzins became the first women admitted to law school in the United States. Both were accepted to Washington University in Saint Louis, Missouri. Instead of completing her degree, Barkaloo decided to take the Missouri bar exam after just one year of school. Even with her studies incomplete, she passed the exam and began practicing law shortly thereafter. However, a fatal case of typhoid fever cut her life short in 1870. Meanwhile, Couzins went on to become the first woman to graduate from a US law school.

More than a century later, women were still fighting for equality in the study and practice of law. In her 1986 book *The Invisible Bar: The Woman Lawyer in America, 1638 to Present*, Karen Berger Morello explores the stories of women such as Mansfield and Barkaloo, as well the struggles of female lawyers today. "There's no question women have made strides in the legal profession," Morello told the *Chicago Tribune*. "But we are still battling an 'invisible bar,' which is the prejudice against women in the profession that keeps them from positions of power."[10]

> "There's no question women have made strides in the legal profession. But we are still battling an 'invisible bar,' which is the prejudice against women in the profession that keeps them from positions of power."[10]
> – *Karen Berger Morello, author of* The Invisible Bar: The Woman Lawyer in America, 1638 to Present

FILLING THE VOIDS LEFT BY WAR

Chauvinistic attitudes toward women in the workplace took a backseat to practical needs during World War I (1914–1918). Many men served as soldiers, leaving behind jobs that needed to be filled as life went on at home. For example, public transportation could not operate without ticket agents. Soldiers' military salaries would be of little use to their families without postal workers, bank tellers, and store clerks back home. Emergencies requiring police and fire departments did not stop happening just because the men were away. Women stepped up to fill all of these jobs.

In addition to all the jobs vacated by soldiers, the war also created many new jobs that needed to be filled—jobs that directly supported the war effort, such as those in munition factories. The soldiers' need for weaponry opened new doors for female factory workers, who before this time had largely been limited to work in textile mills. Many men saw the production of fabric items as a woman's industry, but these men often insisted that they were more qualified than women to manufacture metal items and machinery. Now, however, the choice was to either adequately arm soldiers with weapons made by women or to leave those soldiers with too few weapons on the battlefield. The nation chose women workers.

When the United States' men left to fight during World War I and World War II, women stepped up to take their jobs. Many of these women worked in factories.

Women also worked in some military jobs during World War I. Some women served as ambulance drivers and cooks, while those trained in nursing cared for the injured. Jane Ann Jones joined the United Kingdom's Women's Auxiliary Corps, a group dedicated to fulfilling noncombat jobs in the military, in 1917. While stationed in Calais, France, Jones worked with many servicemen who saw her as more of a nuisance than helpful.

In a recording made by her daughter years after the war ended, Jones recalled her experience in the army. Although she was put in charge of organizing the office, none of the men would listen to her. Finally, in a desperate attempt to make progress, she told her sergeant-major that she needed a new staff made up of men who weren't so set in their ways of doing things. Surprisingly, he approved Jones's request. Jones described the change: "So one by one, within two or three days, the whole office was changed, and I had men who didn't know the job or didn't even think they knew how to do the job and they had to ask me how to do it, so I soon got the office straight, you know, having no one to tell me off or ignore me."[11] After the war, Jones was rewarded for her hard work with an OBE, Officer of the Most Excellent Order of the British Empire, an honor awarded by the King or Queen of England.

When soldiers returned home after the war's end, most of the women who had stepped up to fill necessary jobs lost their employment. Although women were still making small strides in the workplace, large numbers of female employees were not seen again until the start of World War II (1939–1945). Just as they did in World War I, women took over many jobs that soldiers left behind. This time around, though, more women joined militaries. Almost 350,000 women served in the US military during World War II. Their jobs included operating radios, repairing airplanes, and training artillery gunners. General Dwight D. Eisenhower, who would go on to become president of the United States, acknowledged the vital role women played in the nation's successful invasion of enemy territory in 1944. "The contribution of the women of America, whether on the farm or in the factory or in uniform, to D-Day was [essential to] the invasion effort," he said.[12]

"The contribution of the women of America, whether on the farm or in the factory or in uniform, to D-Day was [essential to] the invasion effort."[12]
– *Dwight D. Eisenhower, president of the United States from 1953 to 1961*

ROSIE THE RIVETER

During World War II, the US government needed women to step into less traditional jobs to support the war effort. One company, Westinghouse Electric, sought to inspire women with a fictional machine shop worker called Rosie the Riveter. On a poster produced by Westinghouse, the now-iconic female character wore a blue work uniform with her hair tied up in a red-and-white, polka-dotted bandana. Rosie held her right arm up, flexing her bicep muscle as a symbol of the strength that women could bring to the workforce. Four short words accompanied the drawing: "We can do it!"

Although Rosie was largely the product of artist J. Howard Miller's imagination, she was based on twenty-year-old Naomi Parker Fraley of Alameda, California. A photographer had taken a photo of Fraley as she worked in a factory, and the photo later inspired Miller. Rosie has since become a symbol of the American woman's contributions to the workforce during World War II, with many people assuming that the poster was displayed in factories throughout the United States during the war. In reality, though, Westinghouse displayed it for just two weeks in 1943 before replacing it with another poster from the series, which overall included at least forty different images to inspire women to get the jobs done. However, the image of Rosie has had a lasting impact, as it is still displayed as a feminist symbol today.

Nursing also remained an important job for female military members, and nurses often worked dangerously close to the front lines. Their dedication was not unlike that of the soldiers themselves. The nurses' skills and ability to remain calm in life-or-death situations saved the lives of many soldiers. Harriet Moore Holmes was a military nurse in Hawaii at the time of the Japanese attack on the US military base at Pearl Harbor in 1941. Despite seeing death all around them, the nurses had to focus their energy on saving the living. Holmes remembered how her roommate, also a nurse, responded when her fiancé, a B-17 pilot, was shot down on that December day. "She was very shook up when she found out he was killed," Holmes said, "but she kept right on working."[13]

WOMEN AND POLITICS

Feminism began to influence the workplace as early as the nineteenth century. During that time, many women—and a small number of men—

worked tirelessly for women's suffrage, which is the right to vote in elections. Although voting would not break down all the barriers women faced in the workplace, it was an important step in the process of leveling the professional playing field. Without a voice in politics, women were far less likely to rid the system of the people and antiquated ideas that were keeping them from the jobs they wanted.

As women were fighting for their right to vote, they were also speaking up in other ways, which helped them forge new career paths. As Howard Zinn explains in his book *A People's History of the United States*, women began writing for magazines and newspapers. Some women even started publications of their own. "Some of the most powerful of them joined the antislavery movement. So, by the time a clear feminist movement emerged in the 1840s, women had become practiced organizers, agitators, speakers," Zinn writes.[14]

> "Some of the most powerful [women] joined the antislavery movement. So, by the time a clear feminist movement emerged in the 1840s, women had become practiced organizers, agitators, speakers."[14]
> – Howard Zinn, author of A People's History of the United States

After the Nineteenth Amendment granted women the right to vote in 1920, women also began running for political office. The first female senator, Rebecca Latimer Felton of Georgia, was appointed to the position in 1922 and served in the Senate for one day, largely as a symbolic gesture to honor her long career in state politics and journalism. Some of the other first women to occupy seats in the US Congress, such as the second female senator, Hattie Wyatt Caraway, received the opportunity after their husbands died while serving in office. Appointments such as these often drew criticism. When then Arkansas Governor Harvey Parnell named Senator Thaddeus Caraway's widow as her husband's successor in 1931, the governor told the press that Hattie Wyatt Caraway was entitled to the honor due to her husband's service. Editors at the *Washington Post* responded by writing,

Hattie Wyatt Caraway (left) became the second female US senator in 1931. She was appointed to fill the senate seat of her husband (right) after his death, but she went on to win the next two elections, keeping her senate seat until 1945.

"Representation in Congress belongs to the people of the Senate. Mrs. Caraway should have been given the appointment of her own merit and not on the basis of sentimentality or family claim upon the seat."[15] Hattie Wyatt Caraway was determined not to go down in history as a political placeholder, however. She decided to run against the male candidates seeking to win the Senate seat from her in the 1932 election. Not only did Caraway win, but she won by a landslide, making her the first woman to be elected, not appointed, to the Senate. Winning reelection again in 1938, Caraway served in the Senate until 1945.

Women would go on to accomplish many firsts in the field of politics over the next several decades. In 1996, President Bill Clinton nominated Madeleine Albright for secretary of state; she was the first woman to serve in this powerful and prestigious position. In 2007, Congresswoman Nancy Pelosi became the first female Speaker of the House, the closest a woman has ever been to the presidency—second in the line of succession after the vice president. And nearly another decade later, Hillary Rodham Clinton became the first female presidential candidate to be nominated by a major political party. Although she lost the race to Donald Trump in November 2016, Clinton's nomination was still a major accomplishment for women in the United States. Before any of these milestones would happen, though, women needed to embark on another crusade.

FEMINISM AND THE WORKPLACE

During the 1960s and 1970s, the feminist movement, also called women's liberation or the women's rights movement, had become more prominent than ever. As more women entered the workplace, more of them realized how unfairly female workers were often treated. Many women were harassed by male coworkers while others were ignored in an attempt to undermine their efficiency. Paid less than their male counterparts and overlooked for promotions, women soon realized that getting through the door was only the first battle they had to fight in the workplace.

In 1967, a major advancement in the feminist movement came when President Lyndon B. Johnson signed an executive order that banned sexual discrimination in jobs connected to the federal government. This meant that the order applied not only to federal government jobs but also to positions in companies that conducted business with the government. It was still a far cry from total equality in the workplace, but it was a significant step towards that much larger goal.

One powerful voice in the feminist movement of this era belonged to Gloria Steinem. As a writer, activist, and cofounder of the iconic

Democrat Nancy Pelosi became the first female Speaker of the House in 2007. She lost that position in 2011 when Republicans gained the majority in the House of Representatives.

Ms. magazine, Steinem still speaks out against the injustices she sees in women's path to equality. In an interview with the *Huffington Post*, Steinem pointed out that the key to equality lies in the same place now that it did in the 1960s—the voting booth. "The voting booth is still the only place that a pauper equals a billionaire, and any woman equals any man,"

Steinem said. "If we organized well from the bottom up—and didn't fall for the idea that our vote doesn't count; an idea nurtured by those who don't want us to use it—we could elect feminists, women of all races and some diverse men, too—who actually represent the female half of the country equally. It's up to us."[16]

"The voting booth is still the only place that a pauper equals a billionaire, and any woman equals any man. If we organized well from the bottom up—and didn't fall for the idea that our vote doesn't count; an idea nurtured by those who don't want us to use it—we could elect feminists, women of all races and some diverse men, too—who actually represent the female half of the country equally. It's up to us."[16]
– Gloria Steinem, activist

CHAPTER TWO
HOW DOES DISCRIMINATION AFFECT WORKING WOMEN?

Working women have come a long way from the days of having only a few career paths open to them. Now, instead of filling in for male workers who are away at war, women are regularly working alongside men in a myriad of jobs, including in the armed forces. The women's rights movement has had an undeniable effect on the way society views women in the workplace, as evidenced by the sheer number of women who now hold jobs. Two-thirds of women in the United States contribute an income to their families; many of these women are the sole breadwinners for their households.

Following the surge of feminism in the 1960s and 1970s, female job applicants were being hired in unprecedented numbers. But these women soon had a new challenge facing them: discrimination in the workplace from their male coworkers and supervisors. Even today, many men believe that women are less capable of performing certain types of work than men. These men are often slow to promote female employees or outright unwilling to do so. Some male bosses refuse to give women

More women than ever are part of the American workforce today. But women still face sexism and stereotypes as they try to move up in their careers.

assignments that would help them improve their chances of moving up in their respective fields. A 2017 study by Pew Research Center showed that about four out of ten working women have been discriminated against in the workplace because of their gender. This widespread discrimination against female employees led to the metaphor of the glass ceiling, an invisible yet seemingly impenetrable barrier to advancement for women in the workplace.

Doreen Lorenzo is the president of Quirky, a product development company in New York. In a 2013 interview with the *New York Times*, Lorenzo said that she views much of the discrimination she sees in

29

the workplace as a form of bullying. At first she tried just ignoring the impediments she faced in her own career, but she now believes that is not the best strategy. "I ignored everything. I never wanted gender to be a reason I did anything or was successful, and so I ignored it all. I just plowed ahead," Lorenzo said. "But I look at our daughters and women, and they're still struggling, and I've decided I've got to talk about this more because it's still an issue. It's not better. There's still a glass ceiling."[17]

> "I never wanted gender to be a reason I did anything or was successful, and so I ignored it all. I just plowed ahead. But I look at our daughters and women, and they're still struggling, and I've decided I've got to talk about this more because it's still an issue. It's not better. There's still a glass ceiling."[17]
> – Doreen Lorenzo, president of Quirky, a product development company

Some acts of discrimination are less obvious than others, but no matter how subtle, any sexist act is discriminatory. Jessica Bennett, author Feminist Fight Club: An Office Survival Manual, explained, "It's not rocket science, and sometimes it almost sounds silly. Taken individually, a man interrupting you when you speak, or somebody saying, 'Is it that time of the month?' or having an idea you put forward attributed to somebody else, can sound small. I've heard it referred to as 'death by a thousand cuts.' [It all] adds up over time, so that's what I'm trying to tackle."[18]

Women face discrimination when they are left out of the extracurricular outings of their male coworkers, such as afternoons spent on a golf course with the boss. Men often discuss time-sensitive work topics—and some even close business deals—in this kind of setting. Men sometimes choose to mentor subordinate coworkers as a result of the friendships formed during these activities, which is yet another way women are often denied the same opportunities as men to further their careers. Some women think the answer to this problem is involving themselves in their bosses' activities of choice. Leslie Andrews and Adrienne Wax have written a book about this subject called Even Par: How Golf Helps

SEXIST DRESS CODES IN THE WORKPLACE

Dress codes in the workplace can be a form of discrimination when the rules are different for men and women. Some companies, for example, require women to wear high-heeled shoes as part of their acceptable business attire. Many women take issue with this kind of policy, insisting that high heels have nothing to do with looking neat or professional, but rather they simply make a woman look sexier by society's standards. Although laws prohibiting gender-biased dress codes differ by country and even by state, women often have to speak up with legal action to prove that a specific dress code requirement violates the law.

Sexist dress codes can even extend to a woman's hairstyle, manicure, or makeup. Many black women have faced discrimination by being told they should not wear their hair in certain styles, including braids, dreadlocks, or simply natural hair. In a 2018 article in *Essence* magazine, Siraad Dirshe wrote, "It is our responsibility as Black women not only to increase our awareness of such discrimination but to also listen to our fellow sisters who may be struggling."

Quoted in Siraad Dirshe, "Black Women Speak Up About Their Struggles Wearing Natural Hair In The Workplace," Essence, *February 7, 2018. www.essence.com.*

Women Gain the Upper Hand in Business. "If the important people and deals were in the swimming pool," Wax said, "I'd say learn how to swim."[19] Not everyone agrees with this approach, however. After all, one can be a skilled golfer and still not get invited to the club with everyone else.

Women also still face discrimination in hiring processes. A 2018 study by Ohio State University found that women who received A grades in school are noticeably less likely to receive callbacks for interviews than female candidates who earned Bs, even though high grades made it more likely for men to receive callbacks. To make matters even more troubling, women with the highest grades were even less likely to receive callbacks than men with the lowest grades in the study. The study's author, Natasha Quadlin, had a theory on the reason for these incongruous findings: "Employers value competence and commitment among men applicants, but instead privilege women applicants who are perceived as likeable."[20] Quadlin thought the employers were relying on gender stereotypes instead of on relevant qualifications to evaluate women.

HARASSMENT OF WOMEN IN THE WORKPLACE

Another discriminatory situation that many women face in the workplace is sexual harassment. Sexual harassment can be exhibited in many ways, including unwelcome compliments or other comments about a person's appearance, unwelcome romantic or sexual advances, or physical contact. While some comments may be well intended, they cross the border into harassment when the recipient is made uncomfortable or when her job is affected by her acceptance or rejection of these actions. Although men can also be the victims of sexual harassment, it is far more common for this problem to affect women. And in many cases, the actions of harassment are not well intended. Sexual harassment can be a deliberate attempt at controlling a subordinate employee. Like other types of discrimination, sexual harassment is illegal, but it can be difficult to prove. This leaves many women wary of reporting incidents. Fear of not being believed is often a concern. Others fear losing their jobs as a form of retaliation for reporting harassment.

Some cases of sexual harassment have been well publicized. When President George H. W. Bush nominated Clarence Thomas for the US Supreme Court in 1991, Anita Hill, a former employee of Thomas's, testified that Thomas had sexually harassed her when he was her boss at the Equal Employment Opportunity Commission. Although Thomas was ultimately still appointed to the Supreme Court, Hill's testimony made history by revealing the prevalent problem of sexual harassment in the workplace. Her willingness to speak about the matter in front of an all-male Senate Judiciary Committee brought the topic to the front pages of newspapers across the nation. Hill's actions helped empower other women in similar situations to speak up. Still, many years later, sexual harassment remains a problem in the workplace.

In 1991, Anita Hill publicly testified that she had been sexually harassed at work by US Supreme Court nominee Clarence Thomas. Although Thomas was still appointed to the Supreme Court, Hill's testimony is considered historic in the way that it brought national attention to the issue of harassment in the workplace.

In July 2016, TV journalist Gretchen Carlson filed a sexual harassment lawsuit against Roger Ailes, the chairman of Fox News. She claimed that he had forced her from her job at the network after she refused his sexual advances. She also asserted that he had ignored her when she told him that other men had harassed her in the workplace at Fox. Although Ailes denied Carlson's claims, the network settled the lawsuit that September for $20 million. In an interview with the *New York Times*, Carlson explained why she decided to move forward with her lawsuit. "I just wanted to stand up for myself, first and foremost. And I wanted to stand up for other women who maybe faced similar circumstances," she said.[21]

TV journalist Gretchen Carlson left Fox News in 2016 and filed a lawsuit against the network's chairman, Roger Ailes. In the lawsuit, Carlson said Ailes had sexually harassed her at work.

Some women tell family members or friends after they experience sexual harassment in the workplace. Some even confront their harassers directly. But, because they fear retaliatory actions such as being fired, many women who are subjected to this serious problem do not report it to their work supervisors. Research shows that only 6 to 13 percent of workers who experience harassment file a formal complaint. Although harassment is illegal, complaints within numerous companies have been handled poorly—or even ignored—by people in charge, such as human resources department staff. Women who are sexually harassed at work also tend to report it less in male-dominated professions, such as the military, and partly because of this, sexual harassment is often more prevalent in these settings.

Reporting sexual harassment can be especially intimidating for women who are just starting out in their careers. Eighty percent of these women choose to leave their jobs within two years rather than filing a complaint following sexual harassment. Ariane Hegewisch of the Institute for Women's Policy Research explained in a 2017 interview with *Elle* magazine that trying to solve a harassment issue by changing jobs often hurts women both professionally and financially. "You kind of have to start back at a lower level of seniority, have to prove yourself again. It may be in a job for an employer that is less interesting or pays less well," Hegewisch said.[22]

Many of the lawsuits filed against sexual harassers are ultimately settled when the harassers or their companies offer the woman a large sum of money to end her case. Typically these cash settlements come with a confidentiality clause stating that the woman cannot speak about the harassment publicly. In many cases, women cannot even disclose the amount of money for which they settled. Following her own lawsuit settlement, Carlson wrote a book called *Be Fierce: Stop Harassment and Take Your Power Back*. In it, she explained how negotiations like this can also hurt victims of harassment in the long run: "Harassers often hide behind arbitration and confidentiality clauses. The public never knows how many charges are filed and secretly resolved. In such cases, the victim may get a few bucks, but forfeits her job, and sometimes her career."[23]

Not all harassment comes in the form of ogling or sexual advances. Men can also harass women in the workplace through various hazing-type behaviors, such as teasing and pranks.

"Harassers often hide behind arbitration and confidentiality clauses. The public never knows how many charges are filed and secretly resolved. In such cases, the victim may get a few bucks, but forfeits her job, and sometimes her career."[23]
– *Gretchen Carlson, journalist*

These behaviors are often dangerous in professions that involve physical labor. In 2017, Susan Chira of the *New York Times* reported that some men have dropped heavy tools on female coworkers, while other men have stranded women at the top of wind turbines. Men have even turned on electrical power before women working on power lines were expecting the electric current to start. Even women in these dangerous situations are often unwilling to report the sexual harassment, despite that it is clearly abusive. Megan Block, an employment attorney in Pittsburgh, Pennsylvania, explained why many women won't speak out even after being exposed to such frightening treatment: "A lot of these blue-collar women, they suffer in silence. They don't have the choice, they don't have the money [for a lawsuit], they don't have the time."[24]

To compound the problem, women who face harassment at work frequently suffer from other problems as a result of their mistreatment. Some women start feeling anxious when it is time to get ready for their shifts, anticipating what might happen after they arrive. This anxiety can spill over into other parts of their lives. Harassment can cause women to suffer from depression or post-traumatic stress disorder (PTSD). It can also lead to physical problems such as headaches, muscle aches, and high blood pressure.

JOBS DOMINATED BY WOMEN NOW

Despite the issues of discrimination and sexual harassment, women are thriving in many fields. Many of the professions that first opened doors for women to enter the workforce, such as teaching and secretarial work, are still dominated by women today. Additionally, women now represent the majority of workers in many other professions. Most daycare providers, florists, and health-care aides are women. Just as laborious jobs are called blue-collar work and office jobs are considered white-collar work, positions that are filled primarily by female workers are often called pink-collar jobs.

Teaching is one career field dominated by women. Such jobs are sometimes called pink-collar jobs. But men do these jobs too, and the pink-collar stereotype becomes problematic when people believe women can only perform pink-collar jobs and men cannot.

Although men can and do perform pink-collar jobs, society often considers these positions to be women's work. One problem with this kind of stereotyping is that it prevents many men from pursuing these jobs. As journalist Claire Cain Miller reported in the *New York Times*, "When men take these so-called pink-collar jobs, they have more job security and wage growth than in blue-collar work, according to recent research. But they are paid less and feel stigmatized."[25] The pink-collar stereotype keeps more women employed in these jobs, but it also perpetuates the flawed idea that pink-collar jobs hold less value than others.

FEMALE EXECUTIVES

Although women now make up nearly half of the workforce, they are still severely underrepresented in the top tiers of most companies. In 2017, women held thirty-two of the CEO positions among *Fortune* 500 companies. While this number, which is only 6.4 percent, may sound discouraging, it was the highest number of female company leaders that had ever appeared on the list. Just one year later, the number fell to twenty-four female CEOs. The number fell even further when Campbell Soup Co. CEO Denise Morrison announced her retirement in 2018.

Retirement was also the reason for several of the other female CEOs' departures between 2017 and 2018, leaving the 2018 list with fewer women. But the decrease in female CEOs must also be attributed to the fact that the women who retired were replaced by men. Only one woman on the list, Meg Whitman, has been the CEO of two different *Fortune* 500 companies, first eBay and then Hewlett Packard Enterprise. Despite the losses of so many female leaders, 2018 saw women take the top spots at four *Fortune* 500 companies: Anthem, Kohl's, Ulta Beauty, and Yum China.

Pink-collar professions provide some of the most important services in modern society. Teaching, for example, has a profound effect on a child's future. According to author and educator Byron Garrett, "Early education—which is generally the teaching of children before the age of eight—is where we really need to focus. Early education should not be seen as optional or a 'nice to do,' but should be viewed as a critical ingredient on the student stairway to success."[26] In 2016, 97.5 percent of preschool and kindergarten teachers were women.

Likewise, nurses fulfill an essential purpose for the public. While doctors ultimately have the most control over a patient's medical care, nurses typically spend more time with patients than doctors do. Although the number of men employed as nurses has tripled since the 1970s, nine out of ten nurses in 2016 were women.

There may be some truth to the idea that women are generally better than men at performing certain types of work, and vice versa. Journalist Neil Howe explained in *Forbes* magazine, "Most pink-collar jobs require right-brain EQ and/or 'flow' dexterity skills—which confer a natural advantage to women."[27] The abbreviation *EQ* stands for *emotional quotient*, a measure of a person's ability to observe, assess, and manage emotions. However, despite the potential advantage that women have in pink-collar jobs, it is a problem when people falsely think these jobs are the only work women can excel at. It's also a problem when the pink-collar stereotype discourages qualified men from working in these fields.

Many people think the term *pink collar* is at best obsolete—and at worst, offensive—in this day and age. In *Time* magazine, journalist Amy Tennery wrote, "Unlike 'white collar' and 'blue collar,' 'pink collar' isn't about education or training or even income—it's a way of telling us who 'should' and who 'shouldn't' have a job."[28] She said the logic behind this phrase is rooted in prejudice because it perpetuates stereotypes regarding which jobs women should have.

Regardless, the professions that fall under the umbrella of pink-collar have expanded a great deal since the days when women first entered the workforce. Today, more women than men work as accountants, human resource managers, and veterinarians. Additionally, almost one-third of men currently looking for work will take jobs that have been dominated by female employees.

Kay Stout, an executive adviser who coaches people about career changes, discourages students from making decisions about their classes based on gender, and she tells them to focus on their interests instead. Young women can become incredible teachers, and they can also become skilled electricians. After interviewing Stout, *U.S. News & World Report* writer David Francis wrote, "Men who have an interest in medicine but don't want to be a doctor should inquire about what it takes to be a nurse. Women who have an interest in science should figure out what needs to be done to become an engineer."[29]

39

CHAPTER THREE
WHAT OTHER CHALLENGES DO WORKING WOMEN FACE?

Along with sexual harassment and discrimination, women face many other challenges regarding their employment. This includes generally being paid less than men, pressures to balance work with family responsibilities, and insufficient coverage on employers' health insurance plans. Although women have made many strides forward in the workforce, these problems persist.

THE WAGE GAP

A major problem that has continued in the workplace is that on average women are paid less than men. This disparity, called the *wage gap*, has gradually improved since women first entered the workforce, but the numbers are still far from equal. In 1820, women on average earned thirty-five cents for every dollar that men made. By 1930, women were making fifty-six cents, and by 1970, the difference had narrowed to sixty cents to a man's dollar. In 2018, women on average made approximately eighty cents for every dollar paid to men.

THE WAGE GAP IN HOLLYWOOD

Lead actors and actresses in films and on television usually make a lot of money for their work. Between June 1, 2016, and June 1, 2017, the ten highest-paid actors in the world made a combined amount of $488.5 million. The top actresses also earned a lot of cash, but it was far less than the men's total—the women made $172.5 million together. In an example of this wage gap, Claire Foy made less money than her costar Matt Smith in *The Crown*, even though Foy played the starring role of Queen Elizabeth II in the popular Netflix series. Actresses on average make just thirty cents on the dollar paid to their male counterparts. Some actors have started taking a stand against this wage gap. Benedict Cumberbatch vowed in 2018 that he would not accept any acting role unless his female costars received equal pay.

It is easy to assume that a rise in women's pay led to the most recent narrowing of the wage gap, but the changing economy may actually have more to do with it. As more and more companies have eliminated high-wage manufacturing jobs, men have suffered losses in their own wages. So, the wage gap may have recently narrowed because of a decrease in men's wages, not an increase in women's.

People who study the wage gap have different theories as to why it still exists. For example, some experts say that women are expected to spend more time taking care of their homes and families while men are simply expected to keep gaining work experience that helps them make more money. Others argue that men and women are paid differently on average because so many of them work in different jobs and career fields. However, many women are still paid less when performing the same jobs as men. It is hard to understand why men and women in the same jobs often make different salaries. The theory about men having more education and experience attempts to offer an explanation, but research shows that women in the United States are now earning more college degrees than men. And in situations in which there is no difference between men's and women's education or work experience, men often still make more money.

THE WAGE GAP BY RACE IN SEVEN US CITIES

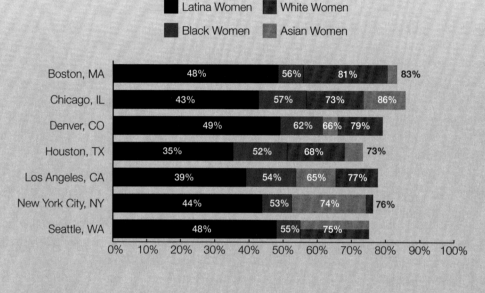

Legend:
- ■ Latina Women
- ■ White Women
- ■ Black Women
- ■ Asian Women

Boston, MA: 48% | 56% | 81% | 83%
Chicago, IL: 43% | 57% | 73% | 86%
Denver, CO: 49% | 62% | 66% | 79%
Houston, TX: 35% | 52% | 68% | 73%
Los Angeles, CA: 39% | 54% | 65% | 77%
New York City, NY: 44% | 53% | 74% | 76%
Seattle, WA: 48% | 55% | 75%

(X-axis: 0% 10% 20% 30% 40% 50% 60% 70% 80% 90% 100%)

Overall, women on average make approximately eighty cents for every dollar that a man makes in the United States. This is a ratio of 80 percent. But the wage gap varies by race and city. This graph shows the average wages of women as a percentage of the average wages of white men in seven cities.

"U.S. Cities Reveal a Wide Range of Gender and Racial Pay Gaps," American Association of University Women, *December 11, 2017. www.aauw.org.*

Some people say that men make more money because they strive to earn high salaries while women focus more on the nonmonetary rewards of their jobs. In her book *Earning It: Hard-Won Lessons from Trailblazing Women at the Top of the Business World*, Joann S. Lublin explained how not making money a priority can be a mistake. "In many cases, women bear a certain responsibility for their pinched pay. They don't get the money they don't ask for," Lublin wrote.[30] In 2014, *Glamour* magazine tackled this topic by asking 2,000 men and women whether they had negotiated for a higher salary upon being hired for a job. The results showed that while 54 percent of the male respondents asked for more money, only 39 percent of the women did. However, research shows that once men and women are in their jobs, they tend to ask for pay raises at the same rate, and women are denied pay raises more often than men.

Another problematic pattern contributing to the wage gap is a formula that many employers use to determine the salaries of new hires. Many interviewers ask prospective job candidates what they were paid in their previous positions. These employers then make job offers based on this information. When women are already making less money than men, perhaps based on their initial salaries being lower, then this strategy from employers simply perpetuates the wage gap.

A math teacher from Fresno, California, helped bring this issue to light when she discovered that she was being paid significantly less than a male coworker who had less education and experience than she did. When Aileen Rizo questioned the reason for the sizeable difference between her paycheck and his—he made $13,000 more—the school shared that its policy was to pay employees based on their previous salaries and that hers had been lower than that of her male colleague. Rizo filed a lawsuit against the Fresno County Office of Education in 2012. She won the lawsuit in 2018. A federal appeals court ruled that employers cannot pay women less than men based on their previous salaries. After the ruling, Rizo said, "We are watching a revolution grow. Women are half the human race. You can't just ignore us. We will no longer let ourselves be paid less, be harassed at work, be assaulted on college campuses and be victims of domestic violence. Our time is now."[31]

The battle against using previous salaries as a justification for paying women less is just part of the wage gap war. Businesses may fall back on other excuses for paying men more money than women for the same work. One of the biggest hurdles for women in fighting wage discrimination is proving that the disparity in their salaries is indeed based on their gender. To win a lawsuit, a woman must be able to prove that the gap between her pay and that of her male counterparts is caused by discrimination based on her gender. It can be especially difficult to prove gender-based discrimination when the discrimination is very subtle, such as when employers' own implicit biases cause them to perceive women as less experienced than men when in fact they have an equal amount of education and experience.

As difficult as it may be to fight the wage gap, the quality of life for many people—not just for women—depends on further progress. Among those affected are family members who depend on women. In her book *The Wage Gap*, Noel Merino wrote, "Lower income for all women, particularly those of color, means less money to support their families with necessities such as housing, food, education, and health care. Closing the pay gap is even more important for women of color who are more likely than their white counterparts to be breadwinners."[32]

"Lower income for all women, particularly those of color, means less money to support their families with necessities such as housing, food, education, and health care. Closing the pay gap is even more important for women of color who are more likely than their white counterparts to be breadwinners."[32]
– Noel Merino, author of The Wage Gap

BALANCING WORK AND MOTHERHOOD

Before women were commonly seen in the workplace, many women who wanted careers felt they had to give up aspects of their personal lives, such as becoming mothers, if they wanted to succeed in the business world. Today, however, many women are working full time while raising children, and they're the primary breadwinners for their households. Some of these women are single or divorced mothers while others are in committed relationships with stay-at-home partners whose primary responsibility is caring for the kids. Still, many other families have two adults who work full time.

One might guess that households with two working parents make double the money of households supported by single mothers, but research reveals an even wider difference. According to the US Census Bureau, two-parent families actually made three times as much as single mothers in 2014. This is likely because fathers generally make more money than mothers due to the wage gap. With so much less money, single mothers often struggle to pay for necessities such as childcare and health insurance.

Even when working mothers have the benefit of a partner's additional income, caring for kids while giving one's best at work can be a challenge. Karen Choi, vice president at an asset management firm, is also a mother of four children. In an interview with the *Guardian*, Choi pointed out, "When your child is sick, has a fever, is throwing up and you are up all night taking care of your child and knowing that the next morning you have to get your other kids to school and then you have to go to work . . . That's when it gets to be very challenging."[33] Balancing work and motherhood isn't always easy, as evidenced by the myriad of news stories, blogs, and magazine articles that advise women on strategies for juggling these two undertakings. While mothers are seen by society as needing to balance work with parenthood, working fathers are rarely

Many women find it challenging to balance their careers with taking care of their families. Society tends to set high expectations for working mothers to balance their careers with parenthood, whereas men are often expected to simply focus on their careers.

pressured to keep that balance in the same way. In an interview with the *Harvard Gazette*, author Lauren Groff refused to answer a question about how she balances writing her novels and short stories with caring for her children: "I understand that this is a question of vital importance to many people, particularly to other mothers who are artists trying to get their work done, and know that I feel for everyone in the struggle. But until I see a male writer asked this question, I'm going to respectfully decline to answer it."[34]

Caring for a family can be even harder for women who can't afford to take time off from work for family needs. The federal Family and Medical

PRIORITIZING CAREER AND FAMILY

Women are placing high-paying careers near the top of their priority lists more than they did in the past. In 1997, 56 percent of women between ages eighteen and thirty-four considered a lucrative career to be one of the most important things in their lives. In 2012, this number had jumped to 66 percent of women in that age range. Research shows that younger women value their careers even more than their male counterparts do. A similar trend was seen in data from older women. In 1997, 26 percent of women ages thirty-five to sixty-four ranked their professional success as important to them, compared with 42 percent of women in this age range in 2012.

One might assume that prioritizing their careers means that women are less concerned with personal endeavors, such as marriage and motherhood, than they were in the past—but this is not the case. Women from both age groups actually ranked being a good parent and having a healthy marriage above success in their careers. It seems that women are not buying into the old-fashioned ideology that they must choose between advancing in their careers and having success in their personal relationships.

Leave Act (FMLA) requires employers that have fifty or more employees within 75 miles (120 km) of an office or worksite to allow workers to take up to twelve weeks off if a family member is dealing with a serious health issue. But this is time off without pay, an important detail for women who cannot afford to go so long without a paycheck. Additionally, women who work freelance do not qualify for FMLA, regardless of the size of the companies for which they work. And FMLA does not protect employees from being fired if they miss work due to a minor health issue. Employment attorney Christina Stoneburner told CBS News, "There is no federal law that mandates employers give consideration to employees with family responsibilities. If your child has a cold, you'll need to take a vacation day or work from home if that's an option for you."[35]

Many working mothers' greatest need for time off is during the months immediately following the birth of a child. The United States is the only industrialized country without a federal law requiring employers to provide their workers with paid maternity leave. This forces many working mothers to choose between their jobs and important bonding time with their infants. FMLA's twelve weeks of unpaid time off applies to new mothers, but many new mothers cannot afford to stay home without pay. Some companies do provide paid maternity leave for their employees, but it is up to individual companies to choose to offer this benefit.

Even when paid maternity leave is available, women often feel pressure to return to work quickly following the birth of a child. Female employees often fear that taking too much time off will negatively affect their careers. In 2015, Marissa Mayer, the CEO of internet company Yahoo, announced that she was pregnant with twins and that she was planning to take limited time off from work. Her decision angered many working women who felt that Mayer, as a high-profile female executive, was contributing to the pressure that many new mothers feel to get back to work as soon as possible after giving birth, regardless of their companies' maternity leave policies. Whether Mayer's critics were right or wrong to fault her, the tendency to judge a working mother's choices is not uncommon in today's society.

Liz Gendreau is an IT program manager who makes a six-figure salary. Her husband is a stay-at-home father to their three children. She and her family are comfortable with this arrangement, but she told *Business Insider* that some people are critical of her role as the breadwinner of their household. They assume she is unhappy or that her husband is threatened by her success. In an article Gendreau wrote for the website, she crushed these misconceptions:

I'm not unhappy. In fact, I'm proud of all my accomplishments. I'm not at all worried about out-earning my husband—I wouldn't want to be married to someone who's bothered by that anyway. I'm not ashamed that I work and he stays at home. To be honest, I'm extremely happy that I can be successful at work, pursue my passions, and have things taken care of at home so I still have plenty of time to be an awesome mom.[36]

The United States is the only developed country without a law that requires employers to provide paid maternity leave. Many new mothers struggle with deciding how much time to take off of work to spend time with their babies, and some can't afford to take any leave from work.

HEALTH INSURANCE AND ACCESS TO BIRTH CONTROL

While some women are balancing work and family, others are concerned with preventing pregnancy or making sure they do not become pregnant until they are ready. Women may struggle more with these concerns if they're unable to access birth control through their employer's health insurance. Until 2012, an overwhelming number of employer health insurance plans would only cover birth control for policyholders after a fee called a copayment was made—despite the fact that the majority of preventive medicines were covered 100 percent. Some plans wouldn't even cover birth control at all. The Affordable Care Act (ACA), known informally as Obamacare, changed this by requiring employers to treat contraception the same as other forms of preventive health care.

Oral contraceptives, also called birth control pills, have had a profound effect on women in the workplace. By providing women with more control over if and when they got pregnant, the birth control pill made it possible for women to enter the workforce without having to worry about how an unplanned pregnancy might affect their careers. As Cecile Richards, former president of the Planned Parenthood Federation of America, explained in an interview with *Fortune* magazine: "If women's careers are interrupted by an unplanned pregnancy, it changes their ability to support themselves, to finish school, to decide when to have a family, and to get a job."[37] In this way, the birth control pill may also be credited with helping working women narrow the wage gap and creating more educational opportunities for women.

"If women's careers are interrupted by an unplanned pregnancy, it changes their ability to support themselves, to finish school, to decide when to have a family, and to get a job."[37]
– *Cecile Richards, former president of the Planned Parenthood Federation of America*

Although the birth control pill was first made widely available to the public in 1960, not everyone welcomed its invention. For religious or other personal reasons, some people oppose the use of birth control. For example, the Catholic Church considers using birth control to be a sin.

When Estelle Griswold and C. Lee Buxton opened a birth control clinic in Connecticut in 1961, they were charged with—and found guilty of—a crime, as it was then illegal to use contraception in that state and several others. Griswold was executive director of the local Planned Parenthood, and Buxton was the chair of the obstetrics department at Yale University.

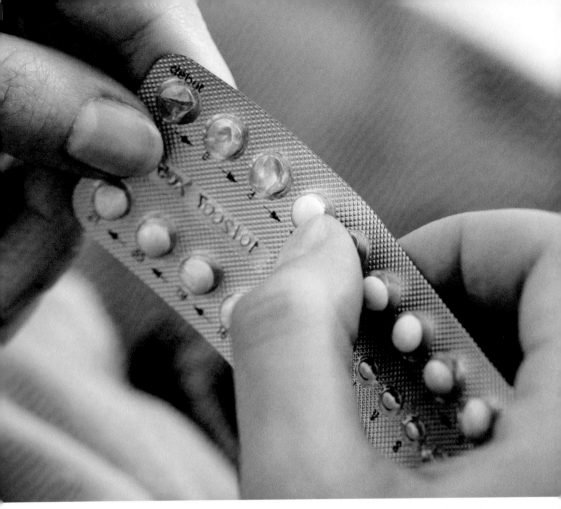

The Affordable Care Act, signed by President Barack Obama, required employers to provide health insurance that covered birth control, including birth control pills. Birth control can help women prevent unplanned pregnancies and plan to get pregnant when they are ready.

They refused to go down without a fight and kept appealing their guilty verdict until their case made it to the US Supreme Court in 1965. The Supreme Court ruled in favor of Griswold and Buxton, making birth control legal for all married women in the United States. Unmarried women, however, were still denied legal birth control until 1972.

The fight to make employer health insurance plans fully cover birth control appeared to be settled when the ACA became law. But when this new health care law required nearly all health insurance plans to cover 100 percent of birth control costs, many conservative politicians worked hard to reverse it. In 2017, President Donald Trump insinuated that the ACA's birth control coverage mandate was an attack on religious freedom. "We will not allow people of faith to be targeted, bullied or silenced anymore," Trump said.[38] He and many other Republican officials agreed that employers should not have to offer insurance that covers birth control if it opposes their religious beliefs. In October 2017, the federal Department of Health and Human Services issued two new rules that offered exemptions to employers who, under the ACA, are required to cover birth control through health insurance. Those rules were stalled by several lawsuits opposing the exemptions. As of 2018, the lawsuits were ongoing.

Critics of Trump's position said that religious beliefs have no place in government matters, including in laws about health insurance coverage. They point out that under the US Constitution, church and state are supposed to be separate entities. Author Jennifer Lawson spoke with CNN after hearing the news about Trump's actions in October 2017.

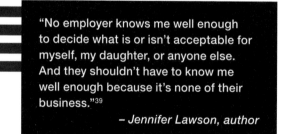

"No employer knows me well enough to decide what is or isn't acceptable for myself, my daughter, or anyone else. And they shouldn't have to know me well enough because it's none of their business."[39]

– Jennifer Lawson, author

"No employer knows me well enough to decide what is or isn't acceptable for myself, my daughter, or anyone else," she said. "And they shouldn't have to know me well enough because it's none of their business."[39]

The issue transcends the debate of whether employers should have to provide insurance that covers birth control for family planning purposes. Doctors prescribe birth control to women for a variety of reasons, including the treatment of serious health conditions such as endometriosis. If a woman with one of these conditions cannot afford to manage it, she is more likely to miss school or work time, or even suffer worse medical problems.

Trump's attempts to alter the ACA's birth control mandate would probably mostly affect women working for smaller businesses, but larger companies with strong religious affiliations could also choose to discontinue coverage of birth control. Because employers would be able to remove just this one part of the health-care coverage—and because that one part relates only to women, denial of birth control coverage could be viewed as a form of discrimination. Sarah Lipton-Lubet of the National Partnership for Women and Families told National Public Radio, "Women shouldn't be denied access to basic health care based on their employers' religious beliefs. We all have the right to our religious beliefs. But the way that this rule treats religion is really an excuse to discriminate."[40]

"Women shouldn't be denied access to basic health care based on their employers' religious beliefs. We all have the right to our religious beliefs. But the way that this rule treats religion is really an excuse to discriminate."[40]
    – Sarah Lipton-Lubet of the National Partnership for Women and Families

CHAPTER FOUR

HOW WILL WOMEN MOVE FORWARD IN THE WORKPLACE?

While working women have made immense progress, there is still a lot of work that needs to be done to achieve gender equality in the workplace. But women have proved themselves up to the challenge. An astounding number of men have been able to cover up sexual harassment in the workplace, but more and more women are realizing that they have a powerful weapon in the fight against this problem— each other. By speaking up and sharing their stories of being harassed, women are working to put an end to this problem. Women are also encouraging each other to be more assertive in the workplace and are developing woman-focused strategies to get ahead professionally. Finally, an increasing number of women are running for political office, where they can help change gender-discriminatory laws and create better opportunities in the workplace for everyone.

THE #METOO MOVEMENT

Sexual harassment in the workplace certainly isn't something new. For years, numerous men have harassed their subordinates in the workplace,

In 2017, the #MeToo and Time's Up movements drew widespread attention to the issues of sexual assault and sexual harassment, including harassment in the workplace. Many women shared their stories online using the hashtag #MeToo to show that countless women have experienced harassment.

and most women have felt powerless about it. Many women have feared that speaking out about harassment would lead to retaliation or that others would not believe them. Many victims of sexual harassment also feel shameful, even though they have done nothing wrong. And the fact that perpetrators are usually in a position of power often makes victims feel as if they have no control over the situation.

However, the power dynamic began to shift in late 2017 when women around the world started using a simple hashtag, #MeToo, to share their experiences of sexual harassment on social media. The #MeToo movement initially gained momentum after several actresses accused high-profile Hollywood movie producer Harvey Weinstein of sexual assault. In an October 2017 *New York Times* article, actress Ashley Judd was among the first people to publicly accuse Weinstein. It wasn't the first time Judd had told someone about Weinstein's behavior, and she wasn't the first woman to accuse him of wrongdoing. She said, "Women have been talking about Harvey amongst ourselves for a long time, and it's simply beyond time to have the conversation publicly."[41] Actress Rose McGowan also said in the *New York Times* article that she had been harassed by Weinstein.

In the days and weeks that followed the publication of the article, dozens of other women, including actresses Salma Hayek and Gwyneth Paltrow, came forward with stories of similar encounters with Weinstein. In May 2018, Weinstein was arrested on criminal charges related to rape and sexual assault. The actresses' willingness to speak out against Weinstein inspired many other women—both within the entertainment field and from a wide variety of other professions—to share how they had been harassed at work. Many famous and powerful men have lost their jobs or faced lawsuits as a result of these accusations.

The phrase "me too" was originally used in this context in 2006 by activist Tarana Burke, who aimed to create support and solidarity for victims of sexual harassment. In 2017, after the public accusations against Weinstein and other famous men, actress Alyssa Milano revived Burke's phrase on Twitter by asking women who have experienced sexual harassment—including sexual assault—to tweet the words "me too." The response was overwhelming. With Facebook users chiming in as well, the #MeToo hashtag went viral. Some users shared their personal stories while others used only the two words that seemed to have started a revolution against sexual harassment. Male victims also revealed their experiences, as harassment can happen to anyone.

Actress Rose McGowan (left) and activist Tarana Burke (right) were two early proponents of the #MeToo movement. Burke introduced the phrase "me too," and McGowan was among the first to publicly accuse Harvey Weinstein of sexual harassment.

The #MeToo movement shed light on the fact that many, many women have quietly endured sexual harassment for a long time. McGowan explained to ABC News how important it was for women to come forward with their stories. "I know they're having nightmares. I know it's really triggering for so many of us out there. It's traumatizing for all of us, you know? But it's so necessary because it's been there all along anyway, whether you want to look at it or not," she said.[42] The #MeToo movement was so groundbreaking that *Time* magazine named its 2017 Persons of the Year "the Silence Breakers," referring to all of the people who came forward with their #MeToo stories to bring long overdue attention to this prevalent issue.[43]

The #MeToo movement led to another collective effort in the fight against sexual harassment: Time's Up, which focuses specifically on sexual harassment in the workplace. Once again, the entertainment industry was the driving force. More than 300 women who work in Hollywood—including actresses Natalie Portman and Reese Witherspoon and television producer Shonda Rimes—came together to identify ways to end sexual harassment in the workplace. One of the first steps was to create the Time's Up Legal Defense Fund to financially help women across all industries who choose to fight back against their harassers in court. Christy Haubegger, a film producer who helped found Time's Up, told *Time* magazine, "Time's Up was founded on the premise that everyone, every human being, deserves a right to earn a living, to take care of themselves, to take care of their families, free of the impediments of harassment and sexual assault and discrimination."[44]

> "Time's Up was founded on the premise that everyone, every human being, deserves a right to earn a living, to take care of themselves, to take care of their families, free of the impediments of harassment and sexual assault and discrimination."[44]
> – Christy Haubegger, film producer who helped found Time's Up

Although the problem of sexual harassment in the workplace is finally being recognized publicly, a lot of work still needs to be done to stop this harassment. The problem extends far beyond Hollywood. Women in all types of jobs need to know what to do if they are being harassed, and, just as importantly, everyone must work toward creating a work environment where harassment doesn't take place at all. In an interview with the *New York Times*, Bettina Deynes of the Society for Human Resource Management offered her perspective on solving the problem:

"When you have an effective H.R. department that is supported by leadership, people feel safe about reporting harassment. It has a lot to do with the type of H.R. department: The motive is not the legal liability, but the culture you want."[45] If the harassment is occurring in a workplace that does not have an effective human resources department or managers who are receptive, women may have to consider seeking legal counsel or reporting the problem to police.

THE LEAN IN MOVEMENT

Sheryl Sandberg, chief operating officer (COO) of Facebook, wrote a book in 2013 called *Lean In: Women, Work, and the Will to Lead*. She also created the Lean In Foundation, a nonprofit organization dedicated to helping women reach their professional goals. The phrase "lean in" has both a literal and figurative meaning—to physically lean in to be seen in business meetings as well as to lean in to a career path, generally leading instead of following. The Lean In movement quickly became a call to action to women to take responsibility for their own successes in the business world.

In 2011, *Forbes* magazine named Sandberg the fifth-most powerful woman in the world, a title that made her feel uncomfortable at first. When people congratulated her, she initially chose to downplay the designation, a behavior that Sandberg's own assistant told her was a mistake. However, as Sandberg pointed out in an interview with National Public Radio, her reaction was not uncommon among women. "When a man does a good job, everyone says, 'That's great.' When a woman does that same thing, she'll get feedback that says things like, 'Your results are good, but your peers just don't like you as much' or 'Maybe you were a little aggressive,'" she said.[46] Sandberg explained that the problem starts long before women even rise to positions of power. Little girls on the playground who act too assertive are often labeled "bossy" while

Sheryl Sandberg, Facebook COO and author of *Lean In*, is seen as highly influential in motivating women to meet their professional goals. However, some say Sandberg's Lean In movement doesn't consider the challenges of all women, particularly low-income women.

assertiveness in boys is considered a healthy personality trait. Girls are taught from a young age that being likeable is more important than being successful—and moreover, that the two qualities, at least for women, are mutually exclusive.

The Lean In movement has affected the way many women see themselves and their careers. In a 2018 article in the *New York Times*, Eliot Kaplan, a former executive at Hearst Publishing, explained that following the publication of Sandberg's book, the dynamics of the job interviews he conducted took a major turn. "Five or six years ago, younger job candidates would accept the first offer given to them. Since then, 90 percent want to negotiate—usually money, but also vacation time, responsibilities and so forth. Some would actually say, 'Sheryl Sandberg says I have to,'" Kaplan said.[47]

Of course, the Lean In movement has also drawn its share of criticism. Some women feel that the movement puts too much emphasis on climbing up the corporate ladder as the only path to personal fulfillment in the workplace. True empowerment comes when a woman does not feel pressured to define success in a single way. *Forbes* writer Kathy Caprino said, "There are women by the millions who want to opt out of corporate life, launch startups, become consultants, or go the solopreneur life. . . . The problem is, now our society is calling that type of behavior 'leaning back,' and that's not a positive trend."[48] The Lean In movement also does not offer much help, if any, to low-income women. Many of these women are already working hard, doing the things that Sandberg has suggested, and they are still struggling to get ahead. Many women, such as those who work as nannies or housekeepers, have no corporate ladder on which to move up.

Although Sandberg would like to see more women in executive roles, she says she wants work conditions to improve for women in all professions. Four years after the Lean In movement began, Sandberg did an interview with *USA Today* in which she acknowledged that there was still a lot of work to be done: "Many of the issues we need to work on are as urgent as ever. We are the only developed country in the world that doesn't have paid maternity leave. The only one. We are one of the only developed countries

"We are the only developed country in the world that doesn't have paid maternity leave. The only one. We are one of the only developed countries in the world that doesn't have paid family leave. That's unacceptable. Two thirds of minimum-wage workers are women. Unacceptable. All of these things need to be fixed."[49]
– *Sheryl Sandberg, Facebook COO and author of* Lean In

in the world that doesn't have paid family leave. That's unacceptable. Two thirds of minimum-wage workers are women. Unacceptable. All of these things need to be fixed."[49]

WOMEN RUNNING FOR POLITICAL OFFICES

The changing dynamics of women in the workplace are the result of many efforts. One of the most impactful efforts is the push to increase women's representation in politics. Laws once prevented women from voting and running for political office. Today, women lawmakers and voters are working toward continuing to change old-fashioned and sexist ideologies that still hold women back. As more women join the ranks of national, state, and local governments, they are opening doors for other female workers, both in politics and in many other fields.

In 2018, women held just one-fifth of the elected positions on Capitol Hill. This number inarguably shows enormous progress from the days of the first elected female senator, Hattie Wyatt Caraway. But it was still far from adequate representation when one considers that nearly 51 percent of the US population is female. By March 2018, a record number of women had filed paperwork to run for Congress or for the governorship of their states. The reasons for these women's campaigns were as diverse as the candidates themselves, but among the biggest motivations were the #MeToo movement and the 2016 election of President Donald Trump. Trump was accused of multiple incidents of sexual harassment during his presidential campaign, and the allegations continued unfolding during his presidency. Fed up with discrimination and harassment, many women were campaigning for political offices to gain a larger voice in running the nation.

However, Jennifer Duffy, who has spent thirty years studying female political candidates, sees these women's campaigns as more than just a reaction to Trump's presidency and #MeToo. "That is all important," Duffy said at a Ready to Run training program, which advises women about running for political office. "But in politics, I think what you're seeing is enormous frustration among women. I think it's frustration that some of the biggest issues in our country, and some of the issues that are very important to women, are not being solved."[50]

Although about three-quarters of the women running for office during the 2018 midterm elections were Democrats, women's representation in politics is

"In politics, I think what you're seeing is enormous frustration among women. I think it's frustration that some of the biggest issues in our country, and some of the issues that are very important to women, are not being solved."[50]
– Jennifer Duffy, political analyst

a bipartisan issue. Female lawmakers from both political parties have worked to address issues that directly affect women, such as sexual harassment in the workplace. For example, even as the 2018 midterm campaigns were still underway, some Democrats and Republicans in the Senate were working together on a bill to prevent accused harassers from using legal contracts called nondisclosure agreements, or NDAs, as a means of getting away with sexual harassment. These agreements, which some companies require their employees to sign as a condition of employment, often state that employees cannot say anything negative about their employers publicly. This bill, introduced by Democratic Senator Kamala Harris and Republican Senator Lisa Murkowski, would make sure nondisclosure agreements exclude issues relating to sexual harassment. The goal is to allow women to report sexual harassment without potential repercussions from their employers. As of July 2018, the bill had not been put to a vote.

Women leaders are still continuing to push for more women to enter government. US Supreme Court Justice Ruth Bader Ginsburg has said that there won't be enough women on the Supreme Court until there are nine female justices—in other words, all women. After all, the court was

Senators Kamala Harris (left) and Lisa Murkowski (right) have proposed a bill that would make sure employers' nondisclosure agreements exclude issues relating to sexual harassment. The goal is to make it easier for women to feel safe reporting incidents of harassment in the workplace.

composed entirely of men for almost two centuries. In a 2018 interview with the *Atlantic*, Ginsburg elaborated, "There is a life experience that women have that brings something to the table. I think a collegial body is much better off to have diverse people of different backgrounds and experience, that can make our discussions more informed."[51]

And diversity is exactly what the candidates of the 2018 midterms offered. For example, both lieutenant governor nominees in Minnesota's governor race were Native American women. The Democratic candidate, state Rep. Peggy Flanagan, is a member of the White Earth Band of

Ojibwe and was serving in the state House of Representatives' Native American Caucus in 2018. Her opponent, Republican candidate Donna Bergstrom, is a member of the Red Lake Nation and previously served in the US Marine Corps as a lieutenant colonel.

In Illinois, registered nurse Lauren Underwood, a Democrat, decided to run for Congress to prevent the incumbent, Republican Randy Hultgren, from reversing the ACA. Underwood served as a health advisor in the Obama administration. In the 2018 Democratic primary election to represent Illinois' Fourteenth District, she won 57 percent of the vote despite being one of seven candidates. She was the only woman and the only African American candidate in the race.

Republican Congresswoman Martha McSally of Arizona couldn't be more unlike Underwood. A 2018 candidate for Senate, McSally is a Trump supporter. She is similar, though, as a trailblazer who has worked to end gender bias. She broke down a gender barrier when she became the highest-ranking female fighter pilot in the US Air Force in 1995. Six years later, McSally made history when she sued then Defense Secretary Donald Rumsfeld over a policy that required women serving in Saudi Arabia to wear a dress-like garment called an abaya over their military uniforms off base. She won that lawsuit, abolishing a gender-biased dress code.

WOMEN WORKING IN STEM FIELDS

As the world moves further into the twenty-first century, jobs in the STEM fields—science, technology, engineering, and mathematics—are becoming more prevalent. Without them, there would be no internet, cell phones, or other advanced technology people use every day. And without new workers entering these fields, future innovation will be limited. In the past, men dominated STEM careers. A widespread belief that male students are inherently better at mastering STEM subjects kept many women from pursuing degrees and jobs in these fields for a long time.

Jobs in STEM are stereotypically considered to be better suited for men, and women have often been discouraged from pursuing these fields. However, many women working in STEM fields today are disproving this stereotype.

But this stereotype is being disproved every day by women who are excelling in STEM fields.

As a professor of biomedical engineering at the New Jersey Institute of Technology (NJIT), Treena Livingston Arinzeh is a pioneer in the field of stem cell research. In 2003, Arinzeh wrote a paper for the *Journal of Bone and Joint Surgery* in which she chronicled how adult stem cells could be harvested from one person and implanted in another. Her findings made history, enabling other medical professionals to use the procedure to help patients. Her work earned her the esteemed Presidential Early Career

Award for Scientists and Engineers from President George W. Bush. Since then, Arinzeh has won numerous other awards for her continued work in the field of biomedical engineering. She also helps other women interested in entering STEM fields. Although Arinzeh believes that women have successfully become more common in these careers, she still tells her female students to make sure they build their professional networks. Attending conferences and making connections at professional events is one way women can help establish themselves as part of their chosen career fields.

Acceptance among male colleagues is one of the largest barriers that many women still face in STEM careers. About half of the women working in these professions report that they have experienced gender discrimination at work. Nancy Steffen-Fluhr, director of the Murray Center for Women at NJIT, shared her views with the *Star-Ledger* newspaper: "Women in science and engineering can easily spend their entire careers on the periphery, far away from the flow of information that powers careers. It's not necessarily the bald discrimination that women faced years ago. It is the small things, the little biases that accumulate into enormous disparities over a career."[52] Working in a sexist environment can have a profound effect on a woman's confidence. Of the women who work in these male-dominated STEM professions, 79 percent say that they feel a need to prove themselves in front of their colleagues. Without the respect of the men, many women believe they cannot make the necessary professional connections to get promoted in STEM careers.

"Women in science and engineering can easily spend their entire careers on the periphery, far away from the flow of information that powers careers. It's not necessarily the bald discrimination that women faced years ago. It is the small things, the little biases that accumulate into enormous disparities over a career."[52]
– *Nancy Steffen-Fluhr, director of the Murray Center for Women at the New Jersey Institute of Technology*

GENDER EQUALITY IN THE WORKPLACE BENEFITS EVERYONE

One factor that makes it difficult for women to advance further in the workplace is that many people see gender equality exclusively as a women's issue. Women in the workplace deserve to be treated fairly, yet it is common for men to shy away from active roles in the solutions to problems such as gender-based discrimination. Many men even worry that they are being blamed for inequality when the subject arises.

But gender equality benefits everyone. When women succeed in the workplace, they are able to contribute more money to their households, which often include men. Historically, industries in which more women work have seen more growth in wages—about a 5 percent increase for every 10 percent of women. Practically speaking, more working women means more money for both men and women. Increasing the number of women in the workplace is good for everyone.

One of the ways in which women can work to reverse this problem is by instilling confidence in female STEM students before they enter the workforce. Pooja Chandrashekar didn't have to focus on building her own confidence—she grew up as the daughter of two engineers who started teaching her about STEM subjects when she was still a child. But when she entered high school, she quickly realized that she was often one of the only girls in her computer science classes. To fix this problem for future high schoolers, Chandrashekar started a tech and computer competition for female middle school students called ProjectCSGIRLS. Similar competitions, workshops, and even summer camps that foster confidence and a love for STEM for girls are becoming increasingly common.

But for women to succeed in STEM careers, businesses need to do more than hire more women; they also need to promote more female employees. Nicole Sanchez, an executive at the web hosting company GitHub, offered her view on how to accomplish this task: "People think diversity is about recruiting and hiring, so they'll stick it over in HR and be done with it. It's usually kept very far away from the CEO. If your mandate is not coming from senior leadership, though, your ability to create a truly diverse staff and an inclusive culture plummets."[53]

Although women have knocked down numerous barriers and celebrated many impressive accomplishments in the workplace over the last century in particular, they cannot become complacent. Doing so would only make it harder to destroy the remaining hurdles that women everywhere must still overcome to achieve true equality in the workplace. No one knows for certain how long it will take to achieve this goal or how exactly it will happen. The only thing that is for certain is that changes in the workplace will continue happening, and working women will undoubtedly be part of that change.

SOURCE NOTES

INTRODUCTION: WORKING WOMEN

1. Ursula Burns, "Ursula M. Burns," *Lean In*, n.d., www.leanin.org.

2. Quoted in Alicia Adamczyk, "Ursula Burns Is the First Black Woman CEO of a Fortune 500 Company. Here's How She Measures Success," *Money*, September 7, 2017. www.time.com/money.

3. Gillian Thomas, *Because of Sex: One Law, Ten Cases, and Fifty Years That Changed American Women's Lives at Work*. New York: St. Martin's Press, 2016, p. 34.

4. Quoted in "Landmark Civil Rights Cases Opened Door for SPLC Official's Law Enforcement Career," *Southern Poverty Law Center*, June 30, 2011. www.splcenter.org.

5. Bryce Covert, "The U.S. Gets Left Behind When It Comes to Working Women," *Forbes*, January 16, 2013. www.forbes.com.

CHAPTER 1: WHAT IS THE HISTORY BEHIND WOMEN IN THE WORKPLACE?

6. Amy Mattsan Lauters, *More Than a Farmer's Wife: Voices of American Farm Women, 1910–1960*. Columbia, MO: University of Missouri Press, 2009, p. 34.

7. Lori D. Ginzberg, *Elizabeth Cady Stanton: An American Life*. New York: Hill and Wang, 2009, p. 23.

8. Quoted in Lucy Kellaway, "The Arrival of Women in the Office," *BBC News*, July 25, 2013. www.bbc.com.

9. Quoted in Sita Khalsa, "Elizabeth Blackwell, M.D.: America's First Female Doctor," *Amazing Women in History*, October 31, 2012. www.amazingwomeninhistory.com.

10. Quoted in "The Battle of the Bar," *Chicago Tribune*, July 19, 1987. www.chicagotribune.com.

11. Quoted in Rachel Obordo and Caroline Bannock, "Women During WWI – Readers' Stories: 'I Can't Do the Work If the Men Won't Listen to Me,'" *The Guardian*, November 10, 2014. www.theguardian.com.

12. Quoted in "History at a Glance: Women in World War II," *The National WWII Museum*, n.d. www.nationalww2museum.org.

13. Quoted in Erica Warren, "Army Nurse Recalls Attack on Pearl Harbor," *San Diego Union-Tribune*, December 7, 2003. www.sandiegouniontribune.com.

14. Howard Zinn, *A People's History of the United States*. New York: HarperCollins, 2003, p. 117.

15. Quoted in "Caraway, Hattie Wyatt," *History, Art & Archives, United States House of Representatives*, n.d. history.house.gov.

16. Quoted in Marianne Schnall, "Exclusive Interview with Gloria Steinem: In Her Own Words," *Huffington Post*, August 12, 2011. www.huffingtonpost.com.

CHAPTER 2: HOW DOES DISCRIMINATION AFFECT WORKING WOMEN?

17. Quoted in Adam Bryant, "Four Executives on Succeeding in Business as a Woman," *New York Times*, October 12, 2013. www.nytimes.com.

18. Quoted in Emma Gray, "How to Fight Subtle Sexism at Work Like a (Lady) Boss," *Huffington Post*, September 16, 2016. www.huffingtonpost.com.

19. Quoted in Jen Doll, "Of Golf Clubs, Boys' Clubs, and Workplace Equality," *The Atlantic*, May 21, 2012. www.theatlantic.com.

20. Quoted in Lucinda Shen, "What's Stopping Female Job Seekers from Landing Interviews? Their 'A' Grades, Says Study," *Fortune*, May 3, 2018. www.fortune.com.

21. Quoted in John Koblin, "Gretchen Carlson, Former Fox News Anchor, Speaks Publicly About Sexual Harassment Lawsuit," *New York Times*, July 12, 2016. www.nytimes.com.

22. Quoted in Bryce Covert, "This Is How Sexual Harassment Ruins Your Career," *Elle*, December 20, 2017. www.elle.com.

23. Gretchen Carlson, *Be Fierce: Stop Harassment and Take Your Power Back*. New York: Hachette Book Group, 2017. p. 33.

24. Quoted in Susan Chira, "We Asked Women in Blue-Collar Workplaces About Harassment. Here Are Their Stories," *New York Times*, December 29, 2017. www.nytimes.com.

25. Claire Cain Miller, "Why Men Don't Want the Jobs Done Mostly by Women," *New York Times*, January 4, 2017. www.nytimes.com.

26. Byron Garrett, "Early Education Can Help Unlock Future Success," *Huffington Post*, November 16, 2015. www.huffingtonpost.com.

27. Neil Howe, "The Spread of the Pink-Collar Economy," *Forbes*, February 28, 2017. www.forbes.com.

28. Amy Tennery, "The Term 'Pink Collar' Is Silly and Outdated—Let's Retire It," *Time*, May 23, 2012. www.time.com.

29. David Francis, "The Pink-Collar Job Boom," *U.S. World & News Report*, September 10, 2012. money.usnews.com.

CHAPTER 3: WHAT OTHER CHALLENGES DO WORKING WOMEN FACE?

30. Joann S. Lublin, *Earning It: Hard-Won Lessons from Trailblazing Women at the Top of the Business World*. New York: HarperCollins, 2016, p. 82.

31. Quoted in Mackenzie Mays, "Fresno Woman Wins Major Court Decision in Her Quest for Equal Pay for Equal Work," *Fresno Bee*, April 9, 2018. www.fresnobee.com.

32. Noel Merino, *The Wage Gap*. Farmington Hills, MI: Greenhaven Press, 2014, p. 130–131.

33. Quoted in Rose Hackman, "Super Boss: Six Women on Juggling Motherhood and Work," *The Guardian*, September 15, 2015. www.theguardian.com.

34. Quoted in Jenna Amatull, "Lauren Groff Says She'll Answer Work-Life Balance Question When Male Writers Get Asked," *Huffington Post*, July 18, 2018. www.huffingtonpost.com.

35. Quoted in Kathryn Tuggle, "Can Family Responsibilities Get You Fired?" *CBS News*, September 3, 2014. www.huffingtonpost.com.

36. Liz Gendreau, "I Have a 6-Figure Job and My Husband Stays Home with the Kids—Here Are 10 Things No One Seems to Understand," *Business Insider*, July 8, 2018. www.businessinsider.com.

37. Quoted in Jaclyn Trop, "50 Years of Legal Birth Control: How It Changed the Workplace for Women," *Fortune*, June 7, 2015. www.fortune.com.

38. Quoted in Robert Pear, Rebecca R. Ruiz, and Laurie Goodstein, "Trump Administration Rolls Back Birth Control Mandate," *New York Times*, October 6, 2017. www.nytimes.com.

39. Quoted in Sandee LaMotte, "Beyond Just Birth Control: Rollback Leaves Some Women Fearful," *CNN*, October 6, 2017. www.cnn.com.

40. Quoted in Alison Kodjak, "Trump Guts Requirement That Employer Health Plans Pay for Birth Control," *National Public Radio*, October 6, 2017. www.npr.org.

CHAPTER 4: HOW WILL WOMEN MOVE FORWARD IN THE WORKPLACE?

41. Quoted in Jodi Kantor and Megan Twohey, "Harvey Weinstein Paid Off Sexual Harassment Accusers for Decades," *New York Times*, October 5, 2017. www.nytimes.com.

42. Quoted in Ashley Louszko, Meagan Redman, and Alexa Valiente, "Rose McGowan Describes Alleged Rape by Harvey Weinstein, Her Thoughts on the Hollywood 'System,'" *ABC News*, January 30, 2018. www.abcnews.com.

43. Stephanie Zacharek, Eliana Dockterman, and Haley Sweetland Edwards, "Person of the Year 2017: The Silence Breakers," *Time*, December 18, 2017. www.time.com.

44. Quoted in Alix Langone, "#MeToo and Time's Up Founders Explain the Difference Between the Two Movements—And How They're Alike," *Time*, March 22, 2018. www.time.com.

45. Quoted in Claire Cain Miller, "It's Not Just Fox: Why Women Don't Report Sexual Harassment," *New York Times*, April 10, 2017. www.nytimes.com.

46. Quoted in Morning Edition, "'Lean In': Facebook's Sheryl Sandberg Explains What's Holding Women Back," *National Public Radio*, March 11, 2013. www.npr.org.

47. Quoted in Judith Newman, "'Lean In': Five Years Later," *New York Times*, March 16, 2018. www.nytimes.com.

48. Kathy Caprino, "Why the Concept Behind 'Lean In' Needs to Be Modified," *Forbes*, March 12, 2015. www.forbes.com.

49. Quoted in Jessica Guynn, "Sheryl Sandberg: Four Years After 'Lean In' Women Are Not Better Off," *USA Today*, March 29, 2017. www.usatoday.com.

50. Quoted in Heather Caygle, "Record-Breaking Number of Women Run for Office," *Politico*, March 8, 2018. www.politico.com.

51. Quoted in Jeffrey Rosen, "Ruth Bader Ginsburg Opens Up About #MeToo, Voting Rights, and Millennials," *The Atlantic*, February 15, 2018. www.theatlantic.com.

52. Quoted in Judy Peet, "Women Engineers and Scientists Still Making Inroads," *Star-Ledger*, March 21, 2010. www.nj.com.

53. Quoted in Emily Moore, "What Do We Need to Get More Women in STEM? 7 Experts Weigh In," *Glassdoor*, May 4, 2017. www.glassdoor.com.

FOR FURTHER **RESEARCH**

BOOKS

Grace Bonney, *In the Company of Women: Inspiration and Advice from Over 100 Makers, Artists, and Entrepreneurs*. New York: Artisan, 2016.

Jennifer Martineau and Portia Mount, *Kick Some Glass: 10 Ways Women Succeed at Work on Their Own Terms*. New York: McGraw-Hill Education, 2018.

Peggy J. Parks, *Sex Discrimination*. San Diego, CA: ReferencePoint Press, 2018.

Jonathan Sposato, *Better Together: 8 Ways Working with Women Leads to Extraordinary Products and Profits*. Hoboken, NJ: Wiley, 2017.

Tarah Wheeler, *Women in Tech: Take Your Career to the Next Level with Practical Advice and Inspiring Stories*. Seattle, WA: Sasquatch Books, 2017.

INTERNET SOURCES

Bryce Covert, "This Is How Sexual Harassment Ruins Your Career," *Elle*, December 20, 2017. www.elle.com.

Charisse Jones, "Pay Gap: 48% of Women Say They Have to Work Twice as Hard as Men to Take Home Half the Pay," *USA Today*, January 18, 2018. www.usatoday.com.

Heather Murphy, "Picture a Leader: Is She a Woman?" *New York Times*, March 16, 2018. www.nytimes.com.

Ai-jen Poo, "How the Fight for Gender Equality Is Changing in 2018," *Time*, March 8, 2018. www.time.com.

Jaclyn Trop, "50 Years of Legal Birth Control: How It Changed the Workplace for Women," *Fortune*, June 7, 2015. www.fortune.com.

WEBSITES

Institute for Women's Policy Research
www.iwpr.org

The Institute for Women's Policy Research is an organization that shares research and information in order to help improve the lives of women from all backgrounds. The organization works to advance women's status through social science research, policy analysis, and public education.

Lean In
www.leanin.org

The Lean In organization was created as a result of Facebook COO Sheryl Sandberg's book *Lean In*. The organization aims to inspire and educate women to help them achieve their professional goals.

Time's Up
www.timesupnow.com

The Time's Up organization, formed by several high-profile women who work in the entertainment industry and the legal field, focuses on ending sexual harassment in the workplace. This includes the Time's Up Legal Defense Fund, which was created to financially help women who choose to file lawsuits or formal complaints against sexual harassers.

INDEX

IMAGE CREDITS

ABOUT THE **AUTHOR**

Tammy Gagne has written dozens of books for both adults and children. Her recent titles include *Women in Engineering* and *Women in Medicine*. She lives in northern New England with her husband, son, and a menagerie of pets.